The
Wit and Wisdom
of
Anon.

The Wit and Wisdom *of* Anon.

Volume 2: Politics

Political Sayings, Anecdotes, and Verse
From the Pen of Anonymous

Compiled by

Marjorie C. Mahoney

Betterway Publications, Inc.
White Hall, Virginia

First Printing: February, 1984

Published by Betterway Publications, Inc.
White Hall, VA 22987

Jacket design by Barbara Wallace
Woodcuts by Marion Reynolds
Typography by Typecasting

Copyright © 1984 by Marjorie C. Mahoney

All rights reserved. No part of this book may be reproduced by any means, except by a reviewer who wishes to quote brief excerpts in connection with a review in a magazine or newspaper.

Library of Congress Cataloging in Publication Data

Main entry under title:
The Wit & wisdom of anon.

    Contents: v. 1. Humor. v. 2. Politics.
    1. American wit and humor.   2. Quotations, English.
I. Mahoney, Marjorie C.   II. Title: Wit and wisdom of anon.
PN6162.W57   1983   827'.008   83-7650
ISBN 0-932620-25-6 (v. 1)
ISBN 0-932620-32-9 (v. 2)

Printed in the United States of America

Dedicated to:
ANON.
"I hate political jokes.
Too many get elected!"

INTRODUCTION

How sad to think that centuries of wit and wisdom have gone unheralded. No anthology of the complete works of Anonymous (also known as "Author Unknown," but hereinafter referred to as just "Anon") has been compiled. Sure, some of Anon's writings have cropped up in various collections, but only fleetingly...never with the respect they deserved. Yet Anon is the most prolific author, poet, dramatist, musician, lyricist, artist, wit, philosopher, theologian, humorist, patriot, educator, lexicographer, etc. of all time.

Let me tell you that my research has yielded thousands of manuscript pages; too much—and too heavy!—for one book. In the first volume, *The Wit and Wisdom of Anon—Humor,* we looked at Anon as a humorist. That tasteful collection represents the "clean" facet of Anon's wit and personality. Someday soon, I may issue a "plain brown wrapper" edition of *The Wit and Wisdom of Anon—Humor—* containing Anon's steamier verses. He has had his ribald moments!

If you read Volume 1 on Humor, you now know that no one knows the exact birthdate or birthplace of Anon. We do know, after exhaustive research in the areas of government and politics, that the first political slogans were discovered on the walls of the cave of Neanderthal Man, 35,000 years B.C. It was Anon who wrote: "We need strong leaders! Vote for AHYA. He has great wisdom and the biggest mouth." Or, "Vote for OOGA for Peaceman [note: this word was later crossed out and replaced with the word "Policeman"]—he's tough, has the biggest club in the cave, and his mother wears Brontosaurus-skin army boots!"

Judging from the happy expression on his face, it appears that he won the election.

Times changed and Anon's writings became more sophisticated. It was Anon who wrote campaign slogans for Moses, when Moses was a candidate for Chairman of the IRM (Israelites Rescue Mission). Anon wrote: "This man's agility is amazing. He can climb mountains easily; his strength allows him to carry huge stone tablets back down mountains; he can create burning bushes without the use of matches; and most important... he has great knowledge in the area of water control!" As you know, Moses won the election.

Politicians, statesmen, and world leaders have consistently called upon Anon for political wit and wisdom. It was Anon who first observed, "Every politician has his price, but some hold bargain sales." To Boss Tweed, Anon said, "When you are run out of town, get up front so folks will think it's a parade." To Mussolini, Anon suggested, "Save face...keep the lower part of it shut!" Anon advised a new candidate: "Keep your words tender and sweet—tomorrow you may have to eat them." To Patrick Henry, Anon warned, "If you thought taxation without representation was bad, you should see it *with* representation." When asked if he had heard a senator's last speech, he answered, "I sincerely hope so!" And a disgruntled Anon said, "We need a law to permit voters to sue candidates for breach of promise."

* * *

I began my own modest collection of anonymous writings when I was a student. I found it advantageous in the preparation of school assignments, term papers, etc. However, as a child performer in the theater, I had written my own special material, and was later able to utilize my growing collection in the preparation of parodies and original material for myself and others.

This volume on politics may serve you in your search for that special retort, profound or profane political statement, or just as an "attention-getter" to display your wit and wisdom. I have put all of Anon's political observations in alphabetical order. You will discover one line may be gently humorous, another bitingly satirical, still another wearily philosophical. A number of the quips, anecdotes, one-liners, and zingers that found their way into my files, and into this collection, have been making the political rounds for years. Some have been around so long they are eligible for pensions...but they are still "working" and still sound new to most of us.

If you find more than a few entries familiar, I congratulate you on your erudition and your already established appreciation of the wit and wisdom of Anon. Those of us who have included Anon on our list of favorite writers have always known it was Anon who said it first and Anon who said it best.

Politicians, statesmen, students, voters, or barflies will find that *The Wit and Wisdom of Anon— Politics* is the ideal book to carry in pocket or purse for immediate reference, or on a desk for easy access. This and subsequent volumes will become as important to you as your dictionary or thesaurus, because whether you are running for office, attending a political rally, at home, office, club meetings, and cocktail parties...you are only as good as your material!

Feel free to use any of the material in this collection. Adopt it as your own and impress everyone with *your* political wit and wisdom. Enjoy!

Marjorie Mahoney
Fowlerville, Michigan

accomplishments

To accomplish something important, two things are necessary: a good idea, and not quite enough time.

§ Accounts Payable

Politician's Petty Cash Book:

Feb.	1.	Ad for secretary	$ 1.90
	3.	New tie	55.00
	4.	Secretary's salary	200.00
	7.	Box of candy for secretary	15.00
	10.	Flowers for secretary	125.00
	11.	Candy for wife	12.50
	15.	Secretary's salary	350.00
	16.	Handbag for secretary	250.00
	17.	Candy for wife	12.50
	22.	Gloria's salary	750.00
	23.	Week-end trip with Gloria	1,500.00
	26.	Rent for Gloria	1,000.00
	27.	Candy for wife	12.50
	28.	Fur coat for wife	10,000.00
	29.	Ad for male secretary	1.90

§ Advice

When listening to political speeches, voters should remember that to get to the "promised land" they must first go through the wilderness.

§ Advice to Politicians

It is hard to speak with sweet reason and logic when your fist is clenched.

Remember the advice of the Mama Whale to the Baby Whale: *Only when you are spouting are you likely to be harpooned!*

From listening comes wisdom; from speaking, repentence.

When alone, guard your thoughts. In the family, guard your temper. In public, guard your words.

Remember the banana. When it left the bunch, it got skinned.

Striking while the iron is hot is fine, but don't strike while the head is hot.

It is short-sighted to be long-winded.

Don't pray for tasks equal to your powers, but for powers equal to your tasks.

It is good to strike the serpent's head with your enemy's hand.

Memory alone is a poor substitute for thought.

If you live wickedly, you can hardly die honestly.

To be always "consistent" is to be frequently wrong.

§ **Anatomy** ─────────────────

In the political anatomy of the United States, the farmer is the backbone, the reformer is the wishbone, and the politician is the jawbone.

§ Anonymous Good Works

The men who went through the streets at night, lighting the gas lamps with a pole, were never seen at the end of the pole but left a light in the darkness.

§ Armaments

I'm afraid the teeth so many nations are arming to are not wisdom teeth.

§ Authority

...makes some politicians grow; others just swell.

§ Average Man

The average man is the guy who has had unusual expenses every month of his life—but expects none next month.

backing

Three out of four persons polled favored his candidacy. Next week they are going to conduct another survey; this time, outside of his immediate family.

§ Balance of Payments

A typical American is a fellow who has just driven home from an Italian movie in his German car. He is sitting on Danish furniture, drinking Brazilian coffee out of an English china cup, and writing a letter on Irish linen paper with a Japanese ballpoint pen...complaining to his Congressman about too much American gold going overseas.

§ Bedfellows

If you always live with those who are lame, you will learn to limp.

§ Bias

Bias and prejudice are great time-savers. Politicians can form opinions without having to get the facts.

§ Bores

We can forgive those who bore us; we cannot forgive those we bore.

§ Brains

Some politicians' brains are like concrete—thoroughly mixed up and permently set.

§ Branches of Government

The four branches of government are: the executive, the legislative, the judicial, and the investigative.

Candidates

He claimed to be the most "promising" candidate. Is there any other kind?

The Congressional candidate seemed about to realize his dream—to serve in the Congress of the United States. One day he traveled to a small community on the campaign trail. Realizing that a candidate's religious denomination was very important, he attempted to find out to what church his audience belonged without having to ask anyone. He came up with the following solution:

"Ladies and Gentlemen, my great-grandmother was a member of the Presbyterian Church [*silence*]; my grandfather was a Methodist [*still silence*]; but my grandmother belonged to the Congregational Church [*cold silence*]. However, I had a great aunt who was a Baptist [*loud cheers*] and [*triumphantly*] I have always followed my great aunt in this respect .

A reporter asked Jones, the opposition party candidate for Mayor, what the main issues of the campaign were.

"Issues?" he replied. "There aren't any great issues, I guess. It's just that Smith has the job and I want it."

The candidate refused to answer questions on the grounds that his answers might tend to eliminate him.

A candidate was visiting an office where they had several computers set up to monitor election returns. He asked the operator of one of the computers to check the projected returns. She came up with the estimated results and said, "The computer says you will win, but that personally *it* would not vote for you."

§ Capitalism

Under Capitalism man exploits man. Under Socialism the reverse is true.

§ Committee

...a body that keeps minutes and wastes hours.

§ Character

A politician goes through life creating both character and reputation. His character will be judged by what he stands for; his reputation by what he has fallen for.

§ Common Market

If you want to flatter anyone, look serious and ask him what he thinks about the future of the Common Market.

§ Communism

If Communism is as wonderful as they say, why don't they take down the iron curtain and put in some picture windows?

§ Compromise

...*a deal in which two people get what neither of them wanted.*

§ Congress

It's a good thing that Moses didn't have to submit the Ten Commandments to Congress for approval.

Even after Congress finally adjourns there will probably still be some things wrong with the country.

Congress is a strange institution. A man gets up to speak and says nothing; nobody listens; then everybody disagrees.

Congress is a legislative body that runs the government like nobody's business.

Taxpayers are relieved when Congress adjourns because Congressmen then start to spend their own money.

§ Congressional Expenses

Next time someone tells you talk is cheap, ask him if he knows how much a session of Congress costs.

§ Congressman

When a Congressman does his duty, he looks forward to it with distaste; does it with reluctance; and boasts about it ever after.

Some members of Congress ought to have their mouths taped instead of their speeches.

In Congress, after all is said and done—more is said than done.

§ Conscience

Senator Claghorn always brags about having a clear conscience. Actually, it's more a case of a very poor memory.

§ Conservative

...one who does not think that anything should be done for the first time.

...one who thinks that the well-to-do should have a square deal, too.

It isn't that Americans are conservative, but that they can't stay mad while they're prosperous.

§ Constituents

"I wouldn't vote for you if you were the Angel Gabriel," expostulated the indignant citizen.

The suave politician replied, "If I were the Angel Gabriel, you wouldn't even be in my precinct."

Constituent: "I want an explanation of your action, and I want the truth!"
Politician: "Well, make up your mind. You can't have both!"

§ Constitution

Americans may be divided into three classes: those who are *for* the Constitution, those who are *against* it, and those who have *read* it.

§ Conventions

. . .where the air is filled with hot speeches, and vice versa.

§ Corruption

Politics is full of sins of omission and commission. The omissions are ignored if the commissions are high enough.

debate

The weaker the argument, the louder the voice, and the stronger the language.

§ Deep Thinking

The only reason some people become lost in thought is because it's unfamiliar territory to them.

§ Defense

There are two things against which there is no adequate defense: the nuclear bomb and stupidity.

§ Demagogue

...a man whose open mouth appeals to people with closed minds.

...a man who pretends to be behind people in order to become their leader.

§ Democracy

...form of government where you are entitled to say what you like and do what you're told.

...a place where we have complete control over how we pay our taxes—cash, check, or money order.

...a place where people can say what they think without thinking.

...a country in which everyone has an equal right to feel superior to the other fellow.

...when everybody is somebody, but nobody is anybody.

In a democracy, when people aren't sure what they want, they vote for something different from what they have.

§ Democrats

America is a land where most citizens vote for Democrats, but hope to live like Republicans.

§ Dilemma

...a politician trying to save both his faces at once.

§ Dictatorship

...a system of government where everything that isn't forbidden is obligatory.

§ Diplomacy

...the ability to take something and make the other fellow believe he is giving it away.

Training for diplomacy should require practice in a little-known underdeveloped country where a few blunders wouldn't show much.

§ Diplomat

...a person who is disarming even though his country isn't.

...one who knows what isn't safe to laugh at.

...one who tries to see how long he can talk without saying anything.

§ Diplomats

Ever wonder why diplomats look so somber and serious all the time? Try smiling with your tongue in your cheek.

When diplomats say they agree in principle, it means that nothing was settled.

§ Disarmament

If the arms race doesn't stop, the human race will.

Disarmament is like a party; no one wants to arrive until everyone else is there.

§ Discrimination

When a minority becomes a majority and seizes authority, it hates minorities.

§ Domestic Affairs

The politician's wife was spending the day in Washington and met her husband for lunch. It being a beautiful day, she insisted that they take a walk and enjoy the beauty of the cherry blossoms. The Senator was greeted in a friendly fashion by a gorgeous blonde. The Senator's wife nudged him and asked him who was the girl. The distraught Senator snapped back at his wife, "Don't bother me! I'm trying to think of some way to explain you to *her!*"

 conomics

Economics is paradoxical; to have national prosperity we must spend, but to have individual prosperity we must save.

Another problem with economics is that there are more ways to get into debt than there are ways to pay it off.

§ Economist

A typical economist is one who writes a 100-page report concluding that in cold weather people use more fuel.

§ Economy

Someday we may find that it hurts just as much to lose your money in the stock market under the S.E.C. as it did in the old unethical days.

§ Education

Americans worry about all the people who can't read or write in the underdeveloped nations, but it's educated people in this country who got us into our present mess.

§ Ego

No one in the world thinks more highly of himself than a man of moderate capacity who was once raised to power.

§ Elections

Both winning and losing candidates get a kick out of an election, but not in the same place.

Truth crushed to earth will rise again, but by that time the votes have already been counted.

An election is a conflict of interests disguised as a contest of principles.

§ Entitlement

A politician died and sought admission at the Pearly Gates.

"Who are you?" asked St. Peter.

"I'm a famous politician."

"What do you want?"

"I want to get in."

"What have you done to entitle you to admission?"

"In addition to public service, I have always tried to help those in need. Just the other day, I saw a poor bag lady and slipped her a dollar."

"Gabriel, is that on the record?"

"Yes, St. Peter, it's entered to his credit."

"What else have you done?"

"Well, when I crossed the street, I saw a poor newsboy half frozen to death, and gave him a whole dollar to get something warm to eat."

"Gabriel, is that on the record?"

"Yes, St. Peter."

"What else have you done?"

"I can't remember anything else just now."

"Gabriel, what do you think we should do with him?"

"Oh, give him back his two bucks and tell him to go to hell!"

§ Entitlements

If the president of the U.S. Chamber of Commerce were ever to write a book about the struggles in Congress over government handouts to states, communities, and special interest groups, we suggest it be called *Mutiny Over the Bounty.*

§ Epitaph

> Here lies a politician.
> Laugh, if you will.
> In mercy, kind providence,
> Let him lie still.
> He lied for his living,
> He lived while he lied;
> When he couldn't lie longer,
> He lied down and died.

§ Errors

If all congressional errors were published like baseball players' statistics, congressmen might perform better.

§ Evolution

It took millions of years to make men out of monkeys, but sometimes it takes only a few minutes to reverse the process.

§ Exercise

The only exercise some politicians get is leaping to conclusions or climbing up and down molehills.

§ Expert

An expert is someone who can tell you tomorrow why the things he predicted yesterday did not happen today.

§ Extravagance

For any government, from economy to extravagance is easy. From extravagance to economy, difficult.

Fair Labor Practices

...for a politician, the practice of hiring someone to do work for which he will get the credit; and if there is a slip-up, having someone on whose desk you can lay the blame.

§ Fame

Those only deserve a monument who do not need one.

§ Federal Aid

...is the system of making money taken from the people look like a gift when handed back.

§ Fence Mending

Some politicians repair their fences by hedging.

§ Fiscal Policy

If Little Bo-Peep lost her sheep today, the government would pay her for not finding them.

§ Foreign Affairs

We apparently hope to bring peace to the world on the installment plan by intervening a little each week somewhere.

Many foreign countries really don't want the U.S. involved in their affairs; they would rather tell us to go home and just leave them a loan.

Some politicians of the western nations who criticize the United States should remember that it's impolite to talk with their mouths full.

§ Foreign Aid

Foreign aid proves that though charity begins at home, it usually ends abroad.

The trouble with foreign aid is that it enables too many countries to live beyond our means.

Whenever a foreign ruler plans a visit to this country, it generally means we are going to come across if he does.

Heaven help us if we discover that other planets are inhabited; think of the increase in our foreign aid.

§ Foreign Policy

The question in this country is whether we should participate in other nations' affairs through our membership in the United Nations Organization or just butt into the world's arguments from time to time.

Our government has a fair to meddling foreign policy.

The trouble with America's foreign relations is that so many of them are broke.

The world is a net. The more we stir in it, the more we are entangled.

§ Free Speech

Free speech is a wonderful thing. We would hate to have to pay to hear some public speakers.

§ Freedom

Freedom is being able to do what you please, without considering anyone except your wife or husband, police, boss, life insurance company, state, federal, and city authorities, and the neighbors.

§ Front Runners

...should remember this: when you are kicked from the rear, it means you are out in front.

God

We should excuse the shortcomings of our politicians. After all, man was made at the end of a hard week's work, when God was tired.

§ Government

Those who think they are going to be happy and prosperous by letting the government take care of them should take a close look at the American Indian.

Another problem government has is that it seems to think the individual owes it a living.

§ Government Employees

Government employees get lots of fringe benefits—a good pension, tenure, health-care benefits, parking space—and the best of all benefits, spending someone else's money. In addition, they receive extra holiday time. For example, people in the private sector don't get off on Columbus's birthday. The reason they celebrate that day in government service is that Columbus started out not knowing where he was going, when he got there he didn't know where he was, and he did it all on borrowed money.

On a government road job, one of the political job holders was assigned to go up the road and warn motorists that the way was partially blocked and to drive carefully. The worker assigned to that duty was afflicted with laryngitis. A motorist drove up and the worker stopped him.

"What's the matter?" asked the motorist.

The worker with laryngitis whispered huskily, "There's a government road job up the road."

"That's all right," whispered the driver. "I'll go by quietly so we won't wake 'em."

 istory ──────────

...an account (mostly false) of events (mostly unimportant).

History proves that war is better at abolishing nations than nations are at abolishing war.

§ **Honesty** ──────────

Party boss to new candidate: "Son, there are two things that are vitally necessary if you are to succeed at politics."

"What are they, sir?"

"Honesty and sagacity."

"What to you mean by 'honesty'?"

"Always...no matter what happens or how adversely it affects you...always keep your word once you have given it."

"And 'sagacity'?"

"Never give it!"

 deal Candidate ─────────

He who knows not, and knows not that he knows not
    Is a fool—shun him.
He who knows not, and knows that he knows not
    Is a child—teach him.
He who knows, and knows not that he knows
    Is asleep—wake him.
He who knows, and knows that he knows
    Is wise—vote for him.

§ Immigration

The answer to: "What is the world coming to?"
is: "America."

§ Inflation

...a fate worse than debt.

...*when nobody has enough money because everybody has too much.*

...what used to cost five dollars to buy now costs ten dollars to repair.

All the talk going around about the high cost of feeding a family is just propaganda put out by people who eat.

§ International Affairs

There's only one man in a million who understands the international situation, and you meet him everywhere.

An international conference is a meeting to decide where the next meeting is to be held.

§ —Isms

Capitalism: If you have two cows, you sell one and buy a bull.
Socialism: If you have two cows, you give one to your neighbor.

Communism: If you have two cows, you give them to the government and then the government gives you some milk.

Fascism: If you have two cows, you keep the cows and give the milk to the government; then the government sells you some milk.

Nazism: If you have two cows, the government shoots you and keeps the cows.

New-Dealism: If you have two cows, you shoot one and milk the other; then you pour the milk down the drain.

§ Issues

When a candidate wants to avoid the facts, he usually discusses great moral issues.

 udgment ———————

The good judgment of some politicians will never wear out. They don't use it often enough.

An astute politician has the good judgment to: be brief, politely; be aggressive, smilingly; be emphatic, pleasantly; be positive, diplomatically; be right, graciously.

§ Justice

*This is the best world that we live in
To lend and to spend and to give in.
But to borrow or beg, or get a man's own,
It's the worst world that ever was known.*

ame Ducks

A lame duck is never so lame that he can't make his way to a new government job.

§ Law

Law cannot persuade where it cannot punish.

One precedent creates another. They soon accumulate and constitute law.

§ Laws

The fact that Congress is no better and no worse than the country is something to worry about. Do we really want to live under laws established by our peers?

Do it now. Tomorrow there may be a law against it.

> Lost is our old simplicity of times,
> The world abounds with laws,
> and teems with crimes.
>
> *(1775)*

§ Leader

...one who has two characteristics: first, he is going somewhere; second, he is able to persuade other people to follow him.

§ Leadership

The trouble with being a leader today is that you can't be sure if the people are following you or chasing you.

§ Legislator

...one who spends half his time making laws and the other half creating loopholes to help his friends evade them.

§ Legislature

...the only school where the recesses are always longer than the sessions.

§ Liberal

...one with both feet firmly planted in the air.

A conservative politician is one who wishes to continue existing evils. A liberal wishes to replace them with others.

§ Limited Warfare

> Don'tcha worry, honey chile,
> Don'tcha cry no more.
> It's just a li'l ol' atom bomb
> In a li'l ol' limited war.
>
> It's just a bitsy warhead, chile,
> On a li'l ol' tactical shell,
> And all it'll do is blow us-all
> To a li'l ol' limited hell.

§ Lincoln

It rarely occurs to politicians that Lincoln is worth imitating as well as quoting.

§ Lying

You can get to the ends of the earth by lying, but you'll never get back.

If George Washington never told a lie, how did he manage to go so far in politics?

Half a truth is a whole lie.

The politician who says "I have never lied to you" just did.

A lie may be a poor substitute for the truth but it is the only one so far discovered.

media

How unfortunate that the only men who know how to run the world become newsmen instead of statesmen.

It's not a bad idea for a politician to remember that no newspaper can misquote silence.

§ Middle of the Road

To keep in the middle of the road one must be able to see both sides.

§ Military Expenditures

It's hard to explain to kids why a nation that spends billions for nuclear bombs is still trying to outlaw firecrackers.

§ Military Spending

Advocates of a strong national defense believe that preparations are less expensive than reparations.

§ Mistakes

With political mistakes, like a lot of other things, it isn't the initial cost... it's the upkeep.

The error of the past is the success of the future. A mistake is evidence that someone tried to do something.

§ Modesty

Those who rate their rank lightly, raise their own dignity.

§ Motives

The noblest motive is the public good.

 ame Calling

The Congressman was well known for his irascible temper and sharp tongue. At one session, he became so angry, he jumped to his feet. "Half of the members of this House are jackasses!"

There arose angry shouts, catcalls, and demands that he apologize immediately.

"All right, I take it back," he grumbled. "Half of the members of this House are *not* jackasses!"

§ National Debt

In a civilized society every generation pays the debts of the last generation by issuing bonds payable by the next generation.

§ Natural Resources

One reason we are such a powerful nation is that we have been unable to exhaust our resources in spite of our best efforts to do so.

§ Naturalized Citizen

...one who becomes a United States citizen with his clothes on.

§ Necessity

Necessity is not only the mother of invention but also serves as a good spur to action. For example, dogs in Siberia are the fastest in the world because the trees are so far apart.

§ Nepotism

"Young man, how long have you been with my office?" asked the Senator.

"Six months, sir," was the answer.

"And how long have you been a page?"

"One month, sir."

"And what are you paid?"

"Three hundred fifty dollars per week, sir."

"Well, I've been watching your work very closely, and I'm very pleased with the progress you have made. I pride myself on recognizing outstanding ability. Therefore, it gives me great pleasure to advise you that beginning next week, you will be my new Administrative Assistant at $55,000 per year."

"Oh boy!...thanks, Dad!"

§ Nuclear War

If the people of the world will not learn to get along without nuclear warfare, nuclear warfare will teach the world to get along without people.

There is only one way to abolish war forever, and that is to have World War III.

World War III will be unique because it will never be mentioned in history books.

Obedience
No one can rule except one who can be ruled.

§ Office Holder

Many an office holder is sworn in one year and sworn at the next.

§ Oldest Profession

A surgeon, an architect, and a politician were arguing as to whose profession was the oldest.

The surgeon said, "Eve was made from Adam's rib, and that surely was a surgical operation."

The architect said, "Maybe, but prior to that, order was created out of chaos, and that was an architectural feat."

The politician said, "Well, who do you think created the chaos?"

§ Open Mind

What the world needs are more open minds and fewer open mouths.

Many an elected official who boasts of having an open mind should have it closed for repairs.

§ Opinion

One of the hardest secrets for a politician to keep is his opinion of himself.

§ Opportunity

Opportunity is often lost by deliberation.

> Four things that never return:
> The spoken word—
> The spent arrow—
> The past life, and
> The neglected opportunity.

The halls of fame are open wide
And they are always full;
Some go in by the door marked "push,"
And some by the door marked "pull."

§ Orators

...should not speak unless by so doing they can improve upon the silence.

...should emulate north woods hunters: they never open their traps more than three times a year.

§ Oratory

...the art of making deep noises from the chest sound like important messages from the brain.

Love, knavery, and necessity make good orators.

parties

Some countries have a different kind of two-party system. There, while one party is in power, the other party is in jail.

§ Partisan Politics

Senator: "I got the vote of every cab driver in the city."

"How did you do that, Senator? Did you give them all a good tip and tell them you were a Democrat?"

"Don't be silly, man. I gave them no tip at all and told them I was a Republican."

§ Party Affiliations

The Sunday school teacher was trying to impress her class of small boys with the omnipotence of the Deity. "Johnny," she asked, "who gives you the clothing, the shoes, the hat you wore this morning?''

''Our President,'' replied Johnny.

The teacher decided to try again. ''Bobby, who gives you meat, bread, milk, and other things to eat?''

''The Secretary of Agriculture.''

The teacher was speechless. *These kids today are supposed to have so much savvy!* She tried again. ''Tommy, who gives you the sun, the stars, and the flowers?''

''God,'' said Tommy.

At last! The teacher smiled happily.

But a little boy next to Tommy grabbed him by the arm and said in a nasty whisper, ''Sit down, you dirty little Republican!''

§ Party Manners

It is an act of good manners when you can yawn without opening your mouth. Something a politician learns early in his career.

If you are at a political dinner party, do not sit next to a legislator. They never pass anything.

§ Party Switching

Young Hopeful: "Sir, what is a traitor in politics?"
Veteran Politician: "A traitor is a man who leaves our party and goes over to the other one."
Young Hopeful: "Well, what is a man who leaves his party and comes over to ours?"
Veteran Politician: "A convert, my boy, a convert!"

§ Patriotism

Patriots should remember that having a preference for their own country does not require their having a prejudice against others.

§ Peace

...a period in which citizens toil to meet the expense of the wars preceding and following.

...a period of cheating between two periods of fighting.

...a short pause between wars for enemy identification.

We will never have world peace until each nation is satisfied with the peace it has.

§ Pentagon

The Pentagon can be a frustrating place to work. For example, an officer, home from strenuous service overseas was assigned to a desk job in the Pentagon. Each day for a week, he shifted the location of his desk, and finally wound up in the men's washroom.

"Must be shell-shocked," other workers reasoned.

But the officer explained: "It's the only place around here where people seem to know what they're doing!"

When a Defense Department official makes a mistake, he often labels it Top Secret *and files it away.*

§ Political Adversity

Adversity introduces a politician to himself.

§ Political Advice

When you stop to think don't forget to start again.

§ Political Banquet

...a plate of cold chicken, carrots, and peas surrounded by warm appeals for donations.

§ Political Bedfellows

Politics makes strange bedfellows, but they soon get accustomed to the same bunk.

§ Political Career

Many a person goes into politics with a fine future and comes out with a terrible past.

§ Political Convention

The only place where a group of important men who can do nothing by themselves save their faces by doing nothing as a group.

§ Political Differences

...*are wholesome. It is political indifference that hurts.*

§ Political Machines

Some politicians are self-made, but most are machine-made.

§ Political Principles

Politics is a struggle between conflicting interests masquerading as a contest of principles.

§ Political Promises

*A promise made
Is a debt unpaid.*

A politician spends half his time making promises and the other half making excuses.

Don't be too dismayed if a politician breaks his promise to you. He probably will replace it with a better one.

§ Political Qualifications

"Whatever became of Junior Jackson?"

"Well," said Uncle Luke, "he tried farming for a spell and failed at that. Then he attended law school but after three years of trying to make a go at law, he failed at that."

"Hey, that's too bad. Junior was always such a good guy. We all like him; in fact, everybody likes him. I'm real sorry to hear that he's such a failure."

"Failure, hell," said Uncle Luke, "he's our Congressman!"

§ Political Speeches

There is a story every political speaker should read before rising to his feet to make a speech. The story concerns a lion who was making his way through the jungle, when it came upon a herd of bulls. The lion sprang upon one of the bulls and killed it, while the other bulls escaped. He took his time feasting upon his kill, roaring with satisfaction after each bite. A hunter in the area heard the lion feasting, found him, raised his gun, and shot the lion dead. What is the moral of this little story? *When you are full of bull, keep your mouth shut.*

§ Politician

...a guy who, if he ain't talking, he ain't listening!

...a person who approaches any subject with an open mouth.

...a person who follows you through a revolving door and comes out ahead of you.

. . . a person with an open mind at both ends.

. . . one who can take something you already know and make it sound confusing.

. . . one who stands for what he thinks the voters will fall for.

. . . a man who divides his time between running for office and running for cover.

. . . a person who keeps the people loyal to him by keeping them angry at someone else.

Nothing can come out of the politician that is not in the man.

The best way to make a politician see the light is to make him feel the heat.

Our politicians should use common sense. The forests would by very quiet if all the birds were quiet except for the best singers.

The man who wants to clean up politics would make a good start by getting out of politics.

§ Politicians

If politicians practiced what they preached, they'd work themselves to death.

It stands to reason that when politicians slap you on the back they are trying to make you cough up something.

Politicians always belong to the opposition party.

Test to determine the career for your child: Place a ten dollar bill on the table to represent a banker. Place a Bible next to it representing a minister. Next to the Bible, a bottle of whiskey, representing a ne'er-do-well. If the child should take all three, he or she will become a politician.

In Biblical days, it was regarded as a miracle if an ass spoke. Boy, have times changed!

The politician has mastered the art of obtaining campaign expenses from the rich to get votes from the poor, on the pretext of protecting each from the other.

You'll find the present crop of politicians surprisingly well versed on all of the big questions of the day, but thoughtful voters should refrain from embarrassing them for the answers.

The average politician is really looking forward to the fall elections. So many things are coming up to be against.

Many a politician with little to offer except an itch for office has been scratched at the polls.

When a politician says that the nation needs a reawakening, it means he is planning to run for office.

There are basically three different types of politicians: the few who make things happen; a larger and interested group who watch things happen; and finally we have the overwhelming majority who have no idea what has been happening.

Politicians are well-known for nepotism. Another term for that is "putting on heirs."

§ Prayer for a Politician

Let me be a little kinder,
Let me be a little blinder
To the faults of those about me,
Let me praise a little more.

Let me be, when I am weary,
Just a little bit more cheery;
Let me serve a little better
Those whom I am working for.

Let me be a little braver
When temptation bids me waver;
Let me strive a little harder
To be all that I should be.

Let me be a little meeker
With the brother who is weaker;
Let me think more of my neighbor
And a little less of me.

§ Prejudice

A good politician is a fellow who has prejudices enough to suit the needs of all his constituents.

§ Presidency

The President is the head of the United States, the Supreme Court is its backbone, and the Houses of Congress are its lungs.

What this country needs is two Presidents: one for the White House, and one for the road.

§ Progress

...what an inactive committee always reports.

Political progress often has little to do with speed, much with direction.

Congressmen generally spend so much time on things that are *urgent* that they have none left over to spend on those that are *important*.

§ Propaganda

...baloney disguised as food for thought.

§ Proverbs

On the day of victory no one is tired.

§ Public Funds

Public money is like holy water; everyone helps himself to it.

§ Public Speaking

Most politicians know how to say nothing. Few know when.

ualifications

Just as spinsters know how to raise other people's children, politicians know how to run other people's business.

§ Quarrel

Political quarrels cannot escape the verdict of public opinion.

§ Quotations

Most effective public speakers know that an apt quotation is often as good as an original remark.

 ebellion

Rebellion to tyrants is obedience to God. *(1776)*

§ Reform

Reform comes from below. No one with four aces ever asks for a new deal.

§ Republican

Then there is the Republican who never condemns inferiority in a Democrat...in fact, he enjoys it.

§ Reputation

No politician is ever as bad as he is painted by his enemies or as good as he is whitewashed by his friends.

It is less difficult to make a mark in politics than to remove one.

Politicians shouldn't be too concerned about what people think of them. Chances are they never think about them at all.

§ Respect

The Mayor of the city returned from a visit to London, England. He reported that the English show great respect and deference to their politicians. "For example," he said, "when the Lord Mayor of London enters a room they call him 'Your Worship.' And when he enters a meeting, a page announces, 'My Lord, the Mayor.' I told my British friends that I too am announced when I enter a room. However, when *I* come in they say: "My God! The Mayor!""

Secret Diplomacy

...is never secret long and rarely diplomatic.

§ Senator

Senators always examine an issue after they've reached a conclusion, and investigate a problem after they've made up their minds.

§ Silence

...is often more guilt than golden.

§ Socialism

...becomes popular whenever hard-working, thrifty people build something worth owning which other people want.

§ Soviet Union

You must give the Russians credit for being considerate. Any trouble they start is always in some other country.

§ Speeches

The politician was complaining to the reporter about the lack of good press coverage during his last speech. "It's a complete conspiracy of silence," he said. "What shall I do?"

The reporter answered: "Join it!"

"Senator Cupperland, nobody could understand your speech on the Federal Reserve System."

"Great! It took me seven hours to write it that way."

> He never knows a thing to say
> Or what to talk about;
> But you must listen long before
> You ever find that out.

It is better for a politician to be quiet and be thought a fool than to speak and remove all doubt.

Most of us like the politicians who give us straight-from-the-shoulder generalities.

Senator: "Have you heard my last speech?"
Voter: "I sincerely hope so!"

What political speeches lack in depth they compensate for in length.

A bemused-looking farmer stood on the steps of the town hall as a political meeting continued inside.

"Do you know who's talking in there now," asked a stranger, "or are you just going in?"

"Nope, I've just come out," said the farmer. "Congressman Smith is making a speech."

"What about?" asked the stranger.

"Well," answered the farmer, "he didn't say!"

He's the kind of politician who thinks twice before he says nothing.

§ Statesman

A politician thinks of the next election. A statesman thinks of the next generation.

A statesman thinks he belongs to the nation, but a politician thinks the nation belongs to him.

§ Statistics

Some government statistics are inaccurate, but those that deal with the cost of living are always on the up and up.

§ Surplus

It's a good thing that money does not grow on trees, or it would be just another surplus commodity for the government to worry about.

act

...a remarkable human quality that lets politicians know just how far to go too far.

...an essential political skill; the knack of letting the other fellow have your way.

...the office holder's ability to make his constituents feel at home when he wishes they were.

§ Taxation

At receptions for the Presidents in the old days, everybody had to approach them with empty hands. Since then, the IRS has made it easier for us to meet that requirement.

Wife: "What is the difference between direct and indirect taxation?"
Husband: "The same as the difference between asking me for money and going through my pockets while I'm asleep."

Taxation is the government's ability to pick the greatest amount of feathers from the goose with the least amount of squawking.

Psychologists tell us that a person should not keep too much to himself. The IRS feels the same way.

§ Taxes

Does it ever seem to you that your payroll check has turned into a receipt for your payroll deductions?

Some day a tax return may contain only three questions:
   1. How much money do you have?
   2. Where is it?
   3. How soon can you get at it?

Capital punishment: the income tax.

This year Congress intends to do something about hidden taxes. They are going to hide them better.

Taxes are the way the government has of artificially inducing the rainy day everybody has been saving for.

If Patrick Henry thought taxation without representation was bad, he should see it *with* representation!

Work hard and pay your taxes cheerfully. Millions of government bureaucrats are depending upon you.

§ Taxpayers

... people who don't have to pass a Civil Service examination to work for the government.

The taxpayer no longer fears that Congress will let him down. He would be happy if it would let him up!

§ Third Parties

Americans are an easygoing people who never stay mad long enough to get a third party well organized.

§ Tolerance

The trouble with being tolerant is that many people think you don't understand the problem.

§ Trust

Trust everybody, but always cut the cards.

§ Truth

Truth never dies. The ages come and go,
The mountains wear away, the stars retire,
Destruction lays earth's mighty cities low;
And empires, states, and dynasties expire.
But caught and handed onward by the wise,
Truth never dies!

Two little girls were talking. Little Lucy said: "A fib is the same as a story, and a story is the same as a lie."

Little Susie answered: "No, it isn't!"

"Yes it is," said Lucy, "because my daddy said so, and my daddy is a professor at the university, and he should know."

"Well, I don't care if he is," said Susie, "my daddy is a Senator, and he knows more about lying than your father does!"

Many politicians have learned that it is better to tell a lie that sounds like the truth than to tell the truth that sounds like a lie.

§ Truthfulness

The main trouble with the "straight and narrow" path is that there's no place to park.

§ Two Kinds of Nations

In one, government policy says, "believe it or not." In the other, it's "believe it or else."

 nions

The state of the Union largely depends on the state of the unions.

§ United Nations

The United Nations spends so much time on procedure that it has no time left to proceed.

The United Nations is the world's stage, with Communism trying to turn it into a puppet show.

§ United States

God looks after fools, drunkards, and the United States.

§ Utopia

...1984 wages...1932 prices...1910 taxes.

 ice President

What we would like to see is a fearless, outspoken candidate for vice president.

The vice president was complaining about losing so many secretaries. "I lost the last one," he said, "because we had so many coffee breaks that she couldn't sleep nights."

The government is the only financial institution which is run with only one vice-president.

§ Virtue

Do not consider any vice trivial and so practice it; do not consider any virtue trivial and so neglect it.

§ Vision

The politician who keeps his ear to the ground may limit his vision.

§ Vote Fraud

"What did the audience do when you told them you had never paid a dollar for a vote?"

"Some of them cheered, but the majority seemed to lose interest!"

"Did you sell your vote?" asked one man of another as they left the voting booth on election day.

"No sir! I voted for that fella because I like him!"

"Oh yeah, I heard he gave you ten dollars."

"Well, when a man gives you ten dollars, it's only natural that you like him!"

Money talks, but campaign money takes care not to tell where it came from.

§ Voter Registration

Citizen: "Is it too late for me to register to vote?"
Registrar: "Which party?"

§ Voters

Some voters never change their opinion because the one they have has been in the family for generations.

We need a law that will permit a voter to sue a candidate for breach of promise.

Voter: "I've heard a great deal about you."
Candidate: "Possibly, but you can't prove any of it!"

§ Voting

"I never vote! It's wonderful to not feel responsible for what goes on in Washington."

 **a r**

War does not determine who is right—only who is left.

Better a bad peace than a good war.

A visitor from another planet could easily pick out the civilized nations. They are the ones with the best implements of war.

The nation that prepares well for war is rarely prepared for peace.

The peace of today costs more than the wars of yesterday.

§ Washington, D.C.

The Washington Monument is one of the very few things in Washington that's always upright.

Washington bureaucrats finally have figured out how to balance the budget—they're going to tilt the country.

Half the politicians in Washington are trying to get investigations started, and the other half are trying to get them stopped.

§ Winning Elections

Lincoln was right, of course. You *can't* fool all the people all of the time. But the winning candidate only has to fool the majority; in a three-candidate race, just a plurality.

§ Working Hours

After a series of all-night sessions, a congressman ran into trouble with his wife, who doubted that he spent all those hours in the House of Representatives. On arriving home very early one morning, he found a note his wife had left for him. It read: "The day before yesterday, you came home yesterday morning; yesterday you came home this morning; so if today you come home tomorrow morning, you will find that I left you yesterday.

§ World War III

I won't print and you won't see
The verses written on World War III.

§ Worry

Up until recent years most of us had always thought we'd fall to pieces before the world did, but it's beginning to look as if it may be a dead heat!

Zeal

There is a holy mistaken zeal in politics as well as in religion. By persuading others, we convince ourselves.

Zeal is fit only for the wise but is more often found in fools and politicians.